Origami

activities

asian arts & crafts for creative kids

Michael G. LaFosse

TUTTLE PUBLISHING

Boston • Rutland, Vermont • Tokyo

First published in the United States in 2003 by Tuttle Publishing, an imprint of Periplus Editions (HK) Ltd., with editorial offices at 153 Milk Street, Boston, Massachusetts 02109.

Library of Congress Cataloging-in-Publication Data

LaFosse, Michael G.
   Origami : Asian arts & crafts for creative kids / Michael G. LaFosse
     p. cm.
   ISBN 0-8048-3497-0 (hc)
   1. Origami--Juvenile literature. I. Title.
TT870.L23426 2003
736'.982--dc21   2003045818

Distributed by

North America, Latin America, and Europe
Tuttle Publishing
Airport Business Park
364 Innovation Drive
North Clarendon, VT 05759-9436
Tel: (802) 773-8930
Fax: (802) 773-6993
Email: info@tuttlepublishing.com
www.tuttlepublishing.com

Japan
Tuttle Publishing
Yaekari Building, 3F
5-4-12 Ōsaki, Shinagawa-ku
Tokyo 141-0032
Tel: (03) 5437-0171
Fax: (03) 5437-0755
Email: tuttle-sales@gol.com

Asia Pacific
Berkeley Books Pte. Ltd.
130 Joo Seng Road
#06-01/03 Olivine Building
Singapore 368357
Tel: (65) 6280-3320
Fax: (65) 6280-6290
Email: inquiries@periplus.com.sg
www.periplus.com

First edition
10 09 08 07 06 05 9 8 7 6 5 4 3 2

Design by Kathryn Sky-Peck
Illustrations by Masturah Jeffrey
Photographs by Richard L. Alexander
Diagrams by Michael G. LaFosse

Printed in Malaysia

contents

The idea of folding materials is an ancient one. Think of the advantages: Folding cloth makes it easy to carry. Folding a letter written on paper keeps its contents secret to the casual passerby. Wrapped in paper, food, medicine, or gifts stay clean and fresh. Documented thoughts, such as stories or journal accounts, are more convenient to carry around and read when the written papers are fanfolded into a book (as opposed to rolling them in long scrolls).

introduction

With origami, the paper becomes more than just a wrapper since the design of the folded paper is interesting in some way. Origami is a special type of paper folding that often results in a beautiful pattern, a representation of a living thing, or a familiar or clever object. In Asia, spiritual symbolism has been expressed through folded paper shapes and forms.

One of the wonderful aspects of origami is its simplicity. The folder does not need anything except something to fold—no glue, no tape, no string or wire—just a piece of paper! Though the materials are simple, origami exemplifies the ability of the human mind to solve problems and create beautiful harmony. Folding is relaxing and peaceful, but it is also fun and exciting to invent new ways to fold paper. The satisfaction of producing a work of beauty, or discovering something, such as a form that you have never seen before, can be addictive. Certain folders specialize in creating origami puzzles, or action models—origami that has moving parts, like the Flapping Bird that moves its wings when its tail is pulled—that delights people of all ages.

The Chinese are credited with the invention of paper, and they were probably the first to create folded paper designs. But today, paper folding is known the world over as *origami*, a Japanese word. There are several possible reasons for this, but perhaps the best involves the Japanese origami crane, one of the most popular designs around the world. This folded paper classic is well documented in Japan's history and has been folded for at least 400 years. For many years the paper crane was considered the most advanced model in the world. When modern publishers and promoters of paper folding needed a simple word for the art, they looked to Japan, the home of the folded paper crane, and came up with origami. In Japanese *ori* means to fold and *kami* means paper.

Since papermaking and paper folding began in Asia, the origami projects presented in this book naturally convey aspects of Asian culture. Flip through these pages and you'll discover a world of chopsticks, Koi fish, and good-luck Darumas!

Paper for Origami

Since origami is simply the art of paper folding, any paper can be used. However, choosing the best paper for a particular project can be as important as the folding process. Here are some things to consider:

Paper for learning and practicing origami does not have to be fancy or expensive. You should look around for papers that are fairly thin and in good supply, like copier paper or discarded magazines. You can fold any of the projects in this book with these papers. You must, of course, prepare your paper by first cutting it to the proper size and shape for the project (the basic techniques are explained in another section of this book). Cut your papers carefully to make perfect squares, and you will be off to a good start.

Once you have learned the folding method for an origami model, and you are able to fold it well, you may decide to make a special example using better paper. There are many beautiful papers to consider.

In the past, you would have probably needed to visit a large city to find art supply stores that sell hundreds of different kinds of papers: machine-made and handmade, in rolls or sheets, and in many colors, patterns, and sizes. Today you can order paper by mail. The Internet has numerous sources of special paper. Suppliers can send orders directly to your mailbox.

Paper folders (people who enjoy making origami) often become paper collectors. Eventually, you may become your best source of special papers if you purchase an extra sheet or two when they are available, or any time you have a little extra money. Paper folders often get together to show one another not only what they have folded, but the papers they have collected from their travels. Handmade paper from exotic lands is a wonderful souvenir, and nothing will be more greatly appreciated by your paper folding friends. If you still cannot find the right paper, try making it yourself! It is not too difficult, and you may be surprised to find information in your library, on the Internet, or perhaps from others in your town who share a similar interest.

Origami Resource Guide

The Origami Source
c/o Phyliss Meth
40-50 166th Street
Flushing, NY 11358
www.origami-usa.org

Sasuga Japanese Bookstore
7 Upland Road
Cambridge, MA 02140
Phone: (617) 497-5460
www.sasugabooks.com
A great source for Japanese books, origami and otherwise!

Origamido Studio
www.origamido.com
The only origami art gallery studio in the United States. Original origami designs and hand papermaking for origami art.

OrigamiUSA
15 West 77th Street
New York, NY 10024
(212) 769-5635
www.origami-usa.org
origami-info@origami-usa.org
A membership supported, not-for-profit, origami dedicated organization

Origami Symbols Key

The folding method for any origami model can be explained using this simple system of drawings and symbols. Most books written from the 1950s through today use this system developed by Akira Yoshizawa, of Japan, and Samuel Randlett, of the United States. Mr. Yoshizawa is widely regarded as the father of modern origami: His origami designs have inspired many of today's great origami artists!

Once you become familiar with the meaning of these symbols, you will be able to learn origami models from any book—even if it is written in another language! Look carefully at the different kinds of lines and arrows pictured on this page. You will see that each symbol has its own meaning, just like musical notation. If you study the origami techniques in the beginning of this book, you will be well prepared for the more advanced projects.

Rotate

Push

X
Follow this spot

Fold in front

Fold behind

Fold and unfold

Turn paper over

Mountain fold

Valley fold

Cut

Crease line

origami techniques

Recognizing Symbols

By making this simple flower bud you will learn how to recognize the following:

- **Valley fold**
- **Mountain fold**
- **Follow this spot**
- **Rotate symbol**
- **Fold and unfold arrow**
- **Fold in front arrow**
- **Fold behind arrow**

1

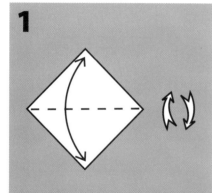

Begin with a square piece of paper, white side up if you are using origami paper. Fold the paper in half, bottom corner to the top corner, and then unfold. Here you see what the valley fold (dashed line) is and what the fold and unfold arrow means. Next, notice the rotate symbol between steps 1 and 2. This means that you must position your paper to look like step 2 before making the next fold.

2

In this case, you must rotate your paper so that the crease made in step 1 is running from the top corner to the bottom corner. Now lift up the bottom corner to make a fold, but do not lift it all the way to the top. See the X, meaning follow this spot, at the bottom corner. You need to look ahead to step 3 to see where the X should go.

3

Fold up the left and right sides. Here there is no X on the left and right sides. Even without the X, it is a good habit to look ahead to the next step, so you will be able to see what the paper should look like.

4

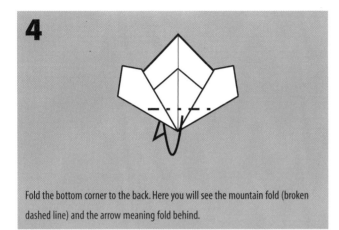

Fold the bottom corner to the back. Here you will see the mountain fold (broken dashed line) and the arrow meaning fold behind.

5

Now you have the finished flower bud! Make several tiny buds from two-inch square papers and paste them onto the front of a handmade card, or save them to decorate your Hashi Wrapper project.

Practicing Neat Folding

Neatness is important when you are folding. This simple exercise will help you practice matching edges—a straightforward task but a common problem for many beginners who do not realize how important it will become later on.

1

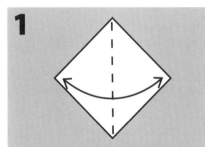

Begin with a square of paper, white side up if you are using origami paper. Fold it in half, corner to corner, then unfold. Be sure to match the corners and the edges of the square carefully before you press the paper flat to make the crease.

2

Fold the two bottom edges to meet at the crease in the center. For neatness, fold only one side at a time. Be sure that the edge of the paper aligns with the crease exactly before you press the paper flat. This shape is often called the kite base. Many origami designs begin from this basic shape.

How did you do? If your shape is not very good, try to figure out what went wrong. Perhaps your paper is the problem. Check to see if it is really square. If the paper is square, perhaps your first fold, from step 1, was done poorly—every fold counts! Try again. Practice will help you improve your basic folding skills. Teaching others what you have learned will improve these skills, too.

3

Fold the kite base in half, from left side to right. This is a good way to check for neatness. Do all of the edges match? Are the corners neat?

4

Make several of these and use them to practice inside-reverse folding, as explained in the next section, where you will make an origami duck!

Learning the Inside-Reverse Fold

In this section you will practice the inside-reverse fold. This is an important origami technique that, with a little practice, will allow you to complete many origami animal designs. The inside-reverse fold is most often used to make bends in the paper for the joints of the limbs, neck, and head of an origami animal.

1

Begin with a kite base folded in half (see the previous section for the folding method). Here you see a typical drawing of an inside-reverse fold instruction. Look at step 4 to see what the paper should look like once it has been inside-reverse folded. Notice that the corner has been bent inside itself.

2

Begin the fold by opening the kite base from underneath. Now you can easily push the narrow end downward. Notice that only part of the kite base will be valley folded, from the bend in the middle to the end of the point.

3

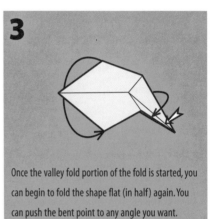

Once the valley fold portion of the fold is started, you can begin to fold the shape flat (in half) again. You can push the bent point to any angle you want.

4

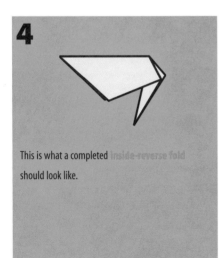

This is what a completed inside-reverse fold should look like.

5

Try adding two more inside-reverse folds, one at the left end and another at the end of the first point. Notice the turn paper over symbol, which tells you that after you make the inside-reverse folds, you should turn the paper over so that it looks similar to the next drawing.

6

This is your finished duck! Make many of them to become an expert at inside-reverse folding.

Making Paper Squares

Most origami projects make use of the square shape as the starting point of design. There are good reasons for this: The square is the easiest shape to make without the use of complicated techniques or special tools, and the shape has a symmetry with many advantages for folded paper design. Other shapes can be used, but they are less frequently encountered. This book uses only square paper designs.

The paper that you are likely to find at hand will not be in the familiar origami square shape. Most paper was made for other purposes such as letter writing, gift wrapping, wall covering, or book, magazine, and newspaper publishing. You can easily prepare such papers for almost any origami project by following these simple steps.

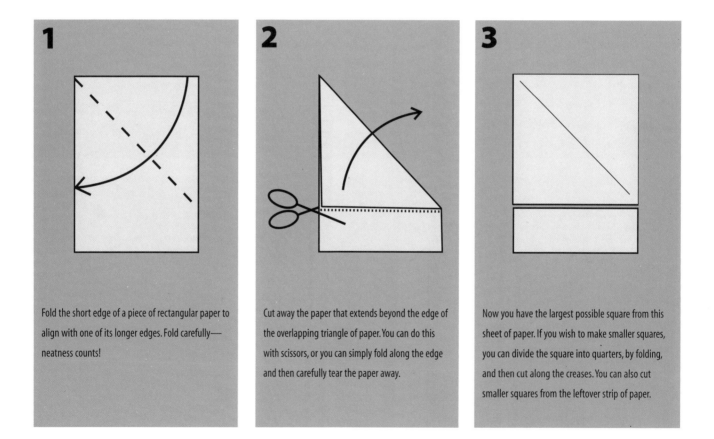

1
Fold the short edge of a piece of rectangular paper to align with one of its longer edges. Fold carefully—neatness counts!

2
Cut away the paper that extends beyond the edge of the overlapping triangle of paper. You can do this with scissors, or you can simply fold along the edge and then carefully tear the paper away.

3
Now you have the largest possible square from this sheet of paper. If you wish to make smaller squares, you can divide the square into quarters, by folding, and then cut along the creases. You can also cut smaller squares from the leftover strip of paper.

4

To make squares from a roll of paper, begin by cutting away a strip as wide as the size square that you will need for your project. Fold and cut a square from this strip in the same way you did with the sheet of rectangular paper.

fan

Regions
of Asia are
hot and humid,
so a fan is an essen-
tial item for comfort
during the hottest time of
the day. People also use fans
to build fires and to dry things.
Long before paper was invented, the
first fans were probably just paddles
fashioned from plant leaves, papyrus, or
bird feathers by people living in the desert.
The first folding paper fans were made in Japan
during the eighth century, and they had important
ceremonial uses.

A folding fan is easily transportable. Its springlike
quality means it nearly opens itself when coaxed, and its
lines have a decorative appeal, making a pleasant display on
a wall or shelf when not in use.

This project is an elegant, self-locking origami
fan, and it is also a great way to practice your essen-
tial folding skills. Small examples serve as chopstick rests. Larger ones can be decorated with
drawings, paintings, writings, or origami—
either before or after folding.

What You Need

Use a square sheet of paper of any size. Small fans,
folded from four- to six-inch (10 to 15 cm) paper,
make good chopstick rests. Larger fans, folded from
ten- to twenty-inch (25 to 50 cm) paper, are nice
for displays or for cooling yourself.

14

What You Do

1

Fold in half, bottom edge to top edge, with the display side (colored or decorated side) on the inside.

2

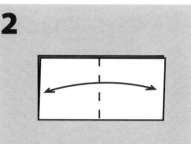

Fold in half, short edge to short edge. Unfold.

3

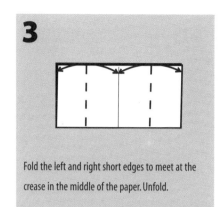

Fold the left and right short edges to meet at the crease in the middle of the paper. Unfold.

4

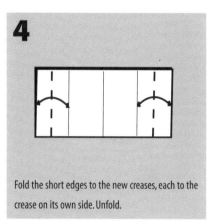

Fold the short edges to the new creases, each to the crease on its own side. Unfold.

5

Fold the right edge to the second crease from the left edge.

6

Your paper will look like this. Unfold.

7

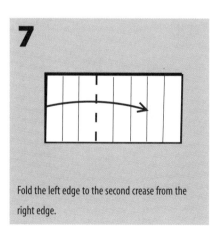

Fold the left edge to the second crease from the right edge.

8

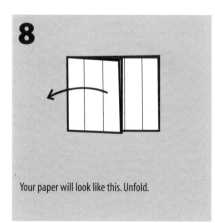

Your paper will look like this. Unfold.

9

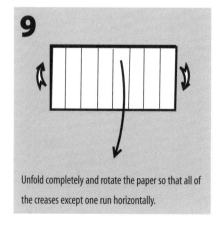

Unfold completely and rotate the paper so that all of the creases except one run horizontally.

10

Fold up the bottom edge to the first crease.

11

Your paper will look like this. Turn the paper over, from left to right, keeping the folded edge at the bottom.

12

Fold up the bottom folded edge, bending the paper at the crease.

13

Your paper will look like this. Turn the paper over, from left to right

14

Fold up the bottom edges and align them with the next crease.

15

Continue turning and folding the paper to make a series of alternating mountain and valley creases.

16

Your paper will look like this.

17

Unfold the top layer of paper.

18

Fold in half, bringing the right edge to the left edge.

19

Fold the left and right bottom corners to the back.

20

Fold up the bottom edge and tuck it into the middle of the fan layers.

21

Open the fan.

For thousands of years, long before metal spoons, forks, and knives existed, chopsticks were the simplest, most practical way to handle food. Today chopsticks, called *hashi* in Japanese, are still commonly used throughout Asia.

In Asia, special attention to the presentation of food and gifts is common, so items are often wrapped. Visitors often remark that many articles are wrapped at least twice! This paper chopstick wrapper is an easy way to keep chopsticks in sets of two. It allows kitchen staff to set a table without handling the ends of the chopsticks that will touch the diner's food or mouth. Formal dining in Asia often features fine-quality chopsticks presented in clean folded paper wrappers. In Asian markets, bags of colorful folded paper chopstick wrappers hang in plastic bags, often with an origami decoration adorning the package.

This design displays the red corner presented against the rest of the white paper, and it is considered a variation of the theme used for the Japanese flag. This makes the white surfaces available for calligraphy or special messages. Most hashi wrappers are folded from rectangles.

hashi wrapper
(chopstick wrapper)

Traditional Japanese design

What You Need

Use paper that is at least six inches (15 cm) square. White paper is most traditional for this wrapper. Origami paper, colored on one side only, is perfect: The wrapper will be white on the outside with a little bit of the colored side showing from inside the top.

What You Do

1

Begin with the colored side up, if you are using origami paper. Fold the bottom edge to the top edge. Unfold.

2

Carefully fold the bottom edge to the crease line and unfold. Repeat with the top edge and unfold.

3

Fold the lower right corner to the center crease. Be careful to align the top edge of the corner with the center crease.

Fold the upper right corner to the first crease from the top. Be careful to align the bottom edge of the corner with this crease.

4

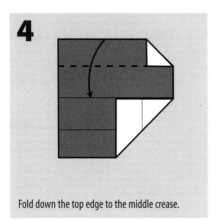

Fold down the top edge to the middle crease.

5

Fold down the top folded edge to the first crease from the bottom.

6

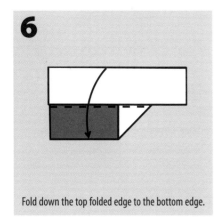

Fold down the top folded edge to the bottom edge.

7

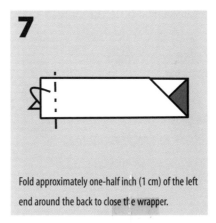

Fold approximately one-half inch (1 cm) of the left end around the back to close the wrapper.

8

The finished Hashi Wrapper.

19

good·luck box

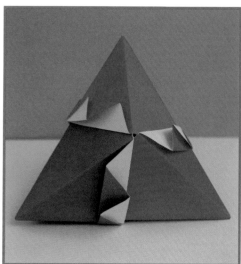

Design by Richard Alexander, based on an origami box by Molly Kahn, U.S.A.

We give gifts for many reasons. Most often we choose something small, but elegant and handmade if possible, as a true expression of goodwill and friendship. Often a gift is a token of a visit—something that the host or hostess can use to remember the wonderful times spent with good friends and relatives.

Gift giving is an integral part of Asian culture as a way to show thanks and appreciation. In many cultures, superstition influences gift giving and offerings of gifts are made to gods in exchange for a bountiful harvest, or simply for good luck. This box is a great way to present a gift of a small piece of jewelry, candy, a seashell, or another item.

This triangular box is a classic design that is versatile as well as beautiful. Molly Kahn first diagrammed this style of box in America in the early 1950s. This variation was designed in 2002 by Richard Alexander, cofounder of the Origamido Studio in Massachusetts. By pressing the polar corners of the box, it splits open in a way that resembles a fortune cookie. These boxes can easily be strung like beads, hung from a mobile, or even placed as ornaments on a tree.

What You Need

You will need three pieces of square paper, each the same size, for this project. Six-inch (15 cm) origami paper is ideal. The most festive boxes are made from papers that are colored differently on each side: You could have up to six different colors on one box! Boxes can be made as large or as small as you like, depending upon the size of the paper you begin with.

What You Do

1

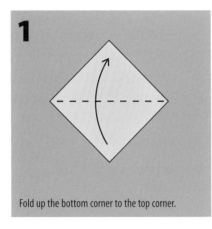

Fold up the bottom corner to the top corner.

2

Fold in half, right corner to left corner, and unfold.

3

Fold up the left and right corners to the top corner.

4

Your paper will look like this. Turn the paper over, from left to right.

5

Fold down the top corner of the top layer, carefully matching with the bottom corner.

6

Fold up the bottom corner of the top layer. Make the corner touch the middle of the folded edge at the center of the paper.

7

Fold up, folded edge to folded edge.

8

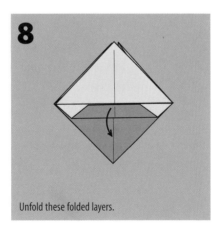

Unfold these folded layers.

9

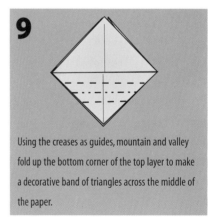

Using the creases as guides, mountain and valley fold up the bottom corner of the top layer to make a decorative band of triangles across the middle of the paper.

10

Bring the two corners away from the back. Mountain fold the vertical center crease to make the unit shape ready for assembly.

11

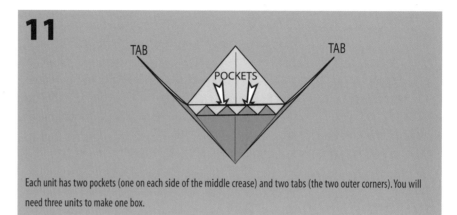

Each unit has two pockets (one on each side of the middle crease) and two tabs (the two outer corners). You will need three units to make one box.

12

Assemble the box by inserting each tab of one unit into one pocket area of another unit. Be sure that all of the valley creases face into the box. If using as a gift box, place a small gift inside after two units are joined. Once all three pieces are arranged, you can push them snugly together to close the box.

The Chinese language takes advantage of homonyms, words that sound alike but mean different things. The Chinese word for bat (*fu*) sounds similar to their word for good fortune (*fu*). For this reason, the image of the bat is commonly seen in Chinese fabrics, drawings, pottery, woodworking, ivory, and other arts. The Chinese consider it good luck if bats roost in your house (maybe because people with bats in their house are less likely to be bothered by insects such as mosquitoes). The Chinese also attach good luck symbolism to the color red, and to the number five, so what could be a better gift than a framed, handmade set of five red bats?

This cute little red bat is fun to make, fun to give, and certainly fun to receive!

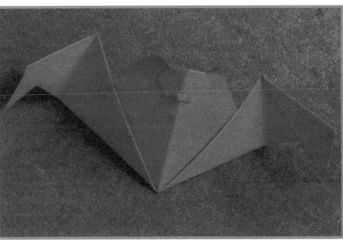

chinese good-luck bat

Design by
Michael LaFosse, U.S.A.

What You Need

Use square paper of any size. If you are using heavy, construction-weight paper, you should fold this bat from a triangle shape. Make a proper triangle by folding a square sheet of paper in half, corner to corner, and then unfolding it. Cut the paper in half along the crease line. You will have two triangles to fold bats from.

Create a bat mobile by attaching thread to your bats and hanging them from sticks or wires.

What You Do

1

Begin with the white side up, if you are using origami paper. Fold up the bottom corner to the top corner.

2

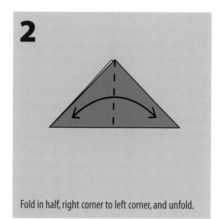

Fold in half, right corner to left corner, and unfold.

3

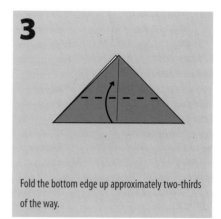

Fold the bottom edge up approximately two-thirds of the way.

4

Your paper will look like this. Turn the paper over.

5

Fold up the left and right halves of the bottom edge. Try to make them touch the intersecting points of the top edges while forming a neat corner at the bottom.

6

Fold down the top edges of the wing papers.

7

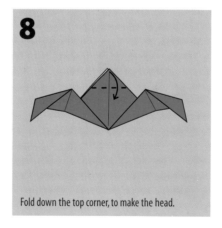

Fold each wing in half. Unfold.

8

Fold down the top corner, to make the head.

9

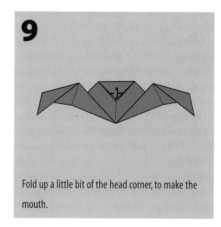

Fold up a little bit of the head corner, to make the mouth.

10

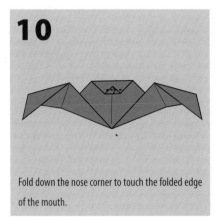

Fold down the nose corner to touch the folded edge of the mouth.

11

Mountain fold the center crease to make the bat more three-dimensional. (Optional: Cut a diagonal slit in the left and right sides of the head paper. Pull up the free corners to make the ears.)

12

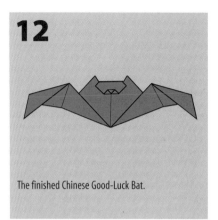

The finished Chinese Good-Luck Bat.

lotus blossom

Traditional Japanese design

Throughout many Asian, Indian, and African cultures, the lotus flower has symbolic connections to religious traditions. In Buddhism, the teachings of Buddha are associated with the lotus because it is thought that the universe has layers without end. In Hinduism, it is believed that the lotus flower blossom emerges from the Hindu god Brahma's navel, and at the center blooms another Brahma. In Yoga, practitioners fold their legs in the lotus position for enhanced meditation because they believe when a person breathes, his or her body expands just as a lotus flower blooms. Since the petals of the lotus flower unfold and emerge from the center, it is often compared to a cycle of continuous renewal.

This lotus requires accurate, repeated folding of the corners to the center, called blintzing. This is a great way to develop folding skills—especially precise, crisp, and symmetrical folds.

What You Need

You will need two pieces of square paper, one large and one small, for this project. The large piece should be at least eight and one-half inches (21 cm) and the small pieces should be six inches (15 cm) or less. The two most popular sizes of origami paper, the nine-and-three-quarter-inch (24 cm) and six-inch (15 cm) size, are ideal. Use thin papers.

What You Do

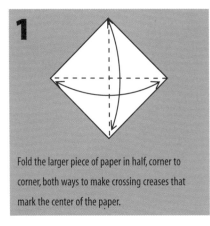

1

Fold the larger piece of paper in half, corner to corner, both ways to make crossing creases that mark the center of the paper.

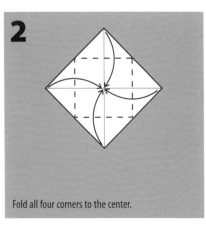

2

Fold all four corners to the center.

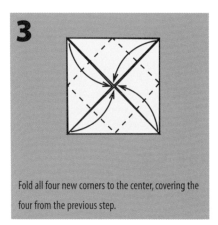

3

Fold all four new corners to the center, covering the four from the previous step.

4

Your paper will look like this. Turn the paper over.

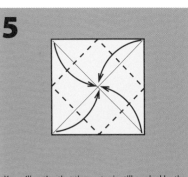

5

You will notice that the center is still marked by the crossing creases. Fold the four corners to the center.

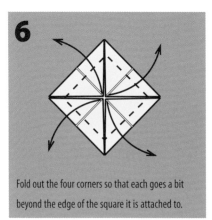

6

Fold out the four corners so that each goes a bit beyond the edge of the square it is attached to.

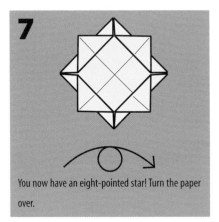

7

You now have an eight-pointed star! Turn the paper over.

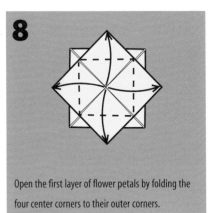

8

Open the first layer of flower petals by folding the four center corners to their outer corners.

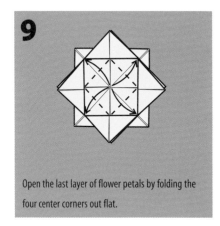

9

Open the last layer of flower petals by folding the four center corners out flat.

10

Lift all eight petals up a little bit to make the flower look fresh and open.

11

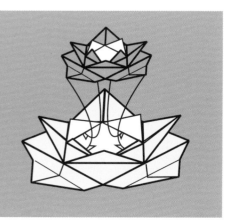

Make a second, smaller lotus blossom, and insert the four bottom corners of the smaller blossom under the folded edges of the center of the larger blossom. They will lock together without the use of glue!

12

The finished Lotus Blossom.

masu box

Traditional
Japanese design

The *masu* is a measuring box. Originally made from wood, it was used traditionally to measure rations of rice and beans. The most ceremonial use of the wooden masu is for drinking sake, a Japanese wine made from rice, especially during their celebration of *Oshogatsu* (New Year's).

This traditional origami box is most often called a masu because it, too, has been used as a measuring box, and it is square like the wooden masu.

We will use the origami masu for the bottom of our three-piece box project. It is perfectly suited for this because it is smooth on the outside, and so the lid will easily slide on. Use any kind of paper, as long as it is the correct size to fit the other pieces of the project. You can use the box alone, however, and if you are folding two, one can serve as a simple lid for the other!

What You Need

Use square paper of any size. Try using colorful papers from magazine covers, gift wrap, old calendars, and scraps of wallpaper.

What You Do

1

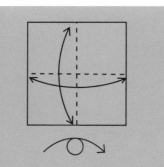

Begin with the colored side up, if you are using origami paper. Fold in half, edge to edge, both ways, to make crossing valley folds on the colored side of the paper. Turn the paper over.

2

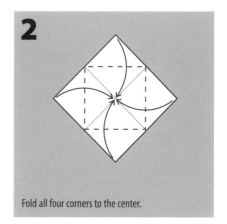

Fold all four corners to the center.

3

Fold the bottom and top edges to meet at the center.

4

Your paper will look like this. Unfold the previous two folds.

5

Fold the left and right edges to meet at the center.

6

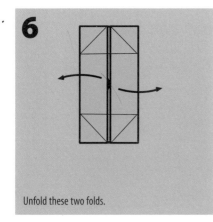

Unfold these two folds.

7

Unfold the left and right corners from the center.

8

Fold the bottom and top edges to meet in the center of the paper.

9

Turn your paper so that it runs the long way, from top to bottom. Open the folded edges from the center. Look at step 10 for the desired shape.

10

Look carefully at the creases in your paper. This folding method has prepared the paper with mountain and valley folds in all of the key places necessary to close up the box shape. Begin by lifting up the left and right walls. Next fold in the four corners a bit.

11

Remember that you are making a square box. Look carefully at the creases and feel how easily they can bend into the right shape.

12

Fold the end flaps up and over the top and bottom walls and into the inside of the box. Lay the corners flat in the bottom of the box.

13

This box needs no glue to keep its shape. Use this box as the bottom to the lotus box project.

shuttle box

Traditionally,
a shuttle is a
wooden spool used to
weave yarn through a
loom. Here it is presented as
a sturdy and easy-to-fold box.
Use this box to hold small items or
to present gifts to friends.

Together the Shuttle Box and the
Masu Box make a beautiful and functional
gift box, or the Shuttle Box can be used in place
of the Masu Box if you prefer this design. Unlike
the Masu Box, this box can be made with rectangles
other than squares. Try making rectangular versions. The
Shuttle Box also contains four slots along the sides that are
perfectly located to accept the flaps produced by our next project, the Lotus Topper.

What You Need

Use any size of square paper. This box makes a
good lid for the Masu Box. Use this box together
with the Lotus Topper to make a decorative box lid.

What You Do

1

Begin white side up, if you are using origami paper. Fold in half, corner to corner, both ways,
to make crossing valley folds.

2

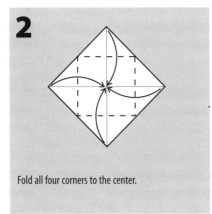

Fold all four corners to the center.

3

Unfold the four corners.

4

Look carefully at the crease pattern. Fold each corner to the crossing crease nearest it.

5

Fold over the four folded edges to make a frame.

6

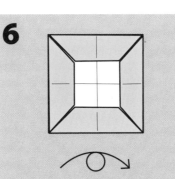

Your paper will look like this. Turn the paper over.

7

Fold the bottom and top edges to meet at the center.

8

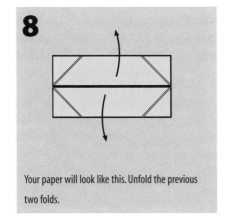

Your paper will look like this. Unfold the previous two folds.

9

Fold the left and right edges to meet at the center.

10

Fold the right top layer to the left like turning the page of a book.

11

Carefully fold over the top and bottom right corners to the center crease.

12

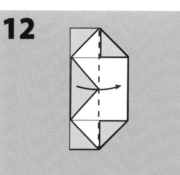

Return the top flap to the right, covering the two folded corners.

13

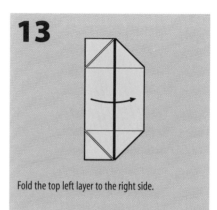

Fold the top left layer to the right side.

14

Fold over the top and bottom left corners to the center crease.

15

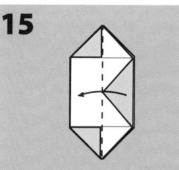

Return the top flap to the left, covering the two folded corners.

16

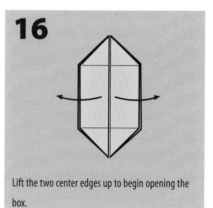

Lift the two center edges up to begin opening the box.

17

Push in the top and bottom corners as you continue to open the box. Sharply mountain fold the outside corners and edges of the box.

18

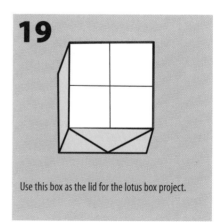

Turn the box over.

19

Use this box as the lid for the lotus box project.

lotus topper

Traditional design,
adapted by
Michael LaFosse, U.S.A.

In Thailand, there is a celebration called *Loy Krathong*, or the Beautiful Water Festival, celebrated during the full moon, late in the fall. Lotus flower-shaped bowls with candles are floated on the water to draw attention to the importance of pure water.

This lotus decoration and lotus-topped box is a versatile decoration for many celebrations.

This lotus-shaped ornament is made using the same principle as the traditional origami lotus project demonstrated earlier in this book. When folded from paper that is the same size as that used for the Shuttle Box, the four base corners will fit like tabs into the pocketlike edges of the box top. This makes for an easy, glueless construction that is very impressive for a gift box.

What You Need

Use square paper of any size. Thin papers work best. To make the full project—a box with a decorative lid—use three same-size sheets of square paper. From one sheet, fold the Masu Box; from another sheet, fold the Shuttle Box; from the third sheet, fold the Lotus Topper. Choose complimentary colors of paper for the three units.

35

What You Do

1

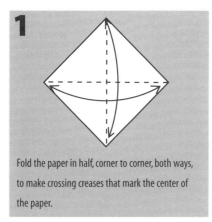

Fold the paper in half, corner to corner, both ways, to make crossing creases that mark the center of the paper.

2

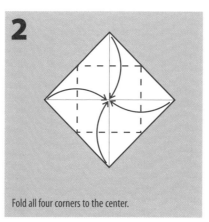

Fold all four corners to the center.

3

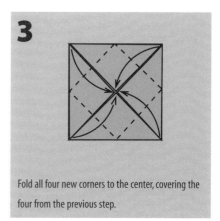

Fold all four new corners to the center, covering the four from the previous step.

4

Your paper will look like this. Turn the paper over.

5

You will notice that the center is still marked by the crossing creases. Fold the four corners to the center.

6

Turn the paper over.

7

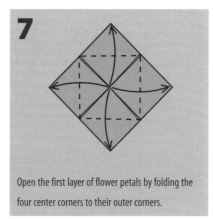

Open the first layer of flower petals by folding the four center corners to their outer corners.

8

Open the last layer of flower petals by folding the four center corners out flat.

9

Lift all eight petals up a little bit to make the flower look fresh and open.

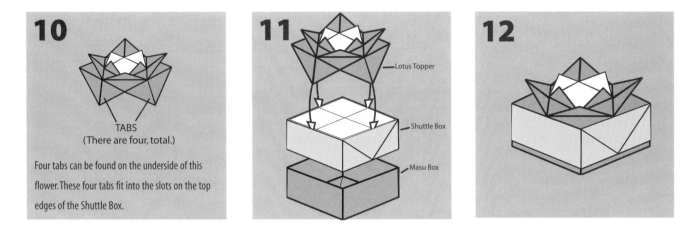

10

TABS
(There are four, total.)

Four tabs can be found on the underside of this flower. These four tabs fit into the slots on the top edges of the Shuttle Box.

11

Lotus Topper

Shuttle Box

Masu Box

12

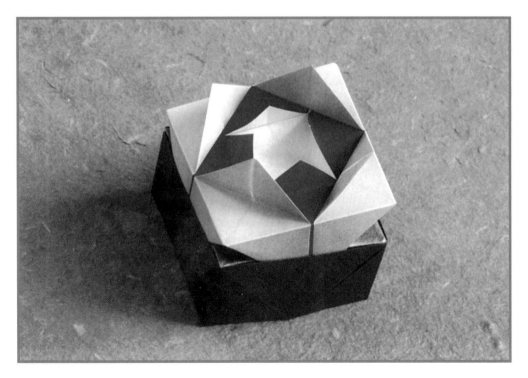

koi

Design by
Michael LaFosse, U.S.A.

Koi is the Japanese word for ornamental freshwater carp, and, like origami, this Japanese word is now recognized all around the world. Originally these fish were called *Nishiki Goi*, a term that referred to fish that were as beautiful as colorful cloth. Over hundreds of years, the Japanese cultivated only the most colorful Nishiki Goi to create the beautiful Koi we know today. Goldfish are also a type of Koi, so you can see that these carp have tremendous, bright colors.

Koi are traditionally displayed during the Boys' Day Festival to symbolize strength. Koi-shaped kites, cloth and paper Koi with streamers, and Koi flags are presented on poles as if they are rising to the top, with the nose, or head, pointing to the sky. This signifies vitality and optimism, as do all of the symbols displayed in the Boys' Day Festival.

What You Need

Use square white paper of any size. The final size of the fish will be approximately half the diagonal length of the square you start with. Decorate your fish with red and black markings after the Koi is folded. Use colored ink, markers, paint, or pencils. These Koi look nice when mounted on a display board covered in suitably colored paper. Combine these Koi with the Lotus to make a pond scene.

What You Do

1

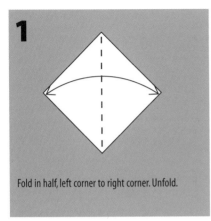

Fold in half, left corner to right corner. Unfold.

2

Fold in the left and right bottom edges so that they are parallel to each other, leaving a gap between them. Look at step 3 for the desired shape.

3

Fold in the top edges to align with the first two edges. Look at step 4 for the desired shape.

4

Fold in half, bottom corner to top corner.

5

Fold in the left and right corners so that they equally overlap, leaving a flat edge at the bottom, not a point. Look at step 6 for the desired shape.

6

Your paper will look like this. Fold out the two corners to make the fins.

7

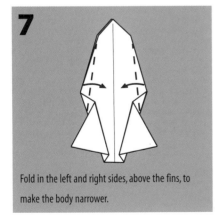

Fold in the left and right sides, above the fins, to make the body narrower.

8

Your paper will look like this. Turn the paper over.

9

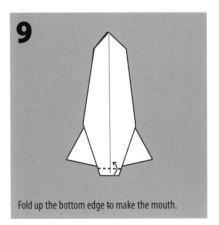

Fold up the bottom edge to make the mouth.

10

Your paper will look like this. (Optional: Follow the details in the close-up to make the barbels on the mouth.)

11

(Mouth detail) Open the triangle shapes, left and right, to make cone shapes. Roll and flatten the cones to extend outward from the mouth.

12

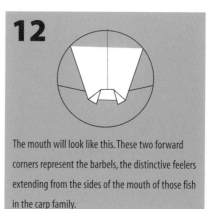

The mouth will look like this. These two forward corners represent the barbels, the distinctive feelers extending from the sides of the mouth of those fish in the carp family.

13

Mountain fold the paper in half lengthwise and turn it sideways to the position shown in step 14.

14

Inside-reverse fold the tail paper (see the folding techniques section in the front of the book for details on this type of fold). Look at step 15 for the desired shape.

15

Inside-reverse fold up the tail paper.

16

Pull down the inside layer of the tail paper to make the lower half of the tail.

17

Optional: Mountain and valley fold the fins, like a fan, to make an attractive shape.

18

Curve the tail fins.

19

The finished Koi.

20

Decorate your origami to resemble your favorite Koi!

The *Kohaku* variety of Koi is a fish that has red markings on a white body. The Tancho Kohaku Koi is a specific design: a white fish with a red spot on its head, so named because it reminds people of the redheaded white bird called a *Toncho*. Since the Japanese national flag is also white with a red circle in the center (symbolizing the rising sun), these fish are popular because they look like swimming flags.

You will note that this project utilizes a scissor cut, not unusual in traditional Asian folded paper figures. We will make use of this traditional technique to create a graceful, forked tail more simply, without the inside-reverse folding we used before. When the final effect is elegant, a cut or two is allowed in traditional, as well as in modern, origami design.

tancho kohaku koi

Design by
Michael LaFosse, U.S.A.

What You Need

Use a square of origami paper, red on one side and white on the other. Any size paper is fine. These Koi are perfect for making a hanging mobile: Attach lightweight thread or fishing line to each Koi, and then hang them from slender sticks of wood or wire.

What You Do

1

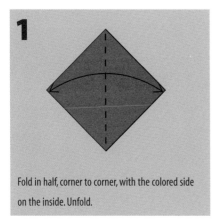

Fold in half, corner to corner, with the colored side on the inside. Unfold.

2

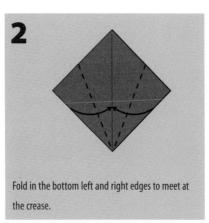

Fold in the bottom left and right edges to meet at the crease.

3

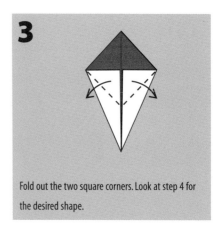

Fold out the two square corners. Look at step 4 for the desired shape.

4

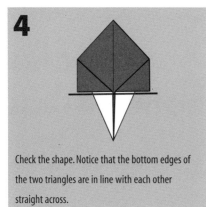

Check the shape. Notice that the bottom edges of the two triangles are in line with each other straight across.

5

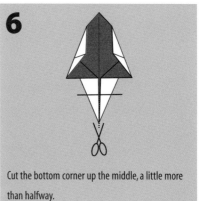

Fold in the left and right edges so that the top halves will be parallel to each other and the bottom halves run straight to the corners of the two fins.

6

Cut the bottom corner up the middle, a little more than halfway.

7

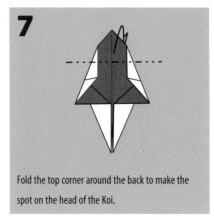

Fold the top corner around the back to make the spot on the head of the Koi.

8

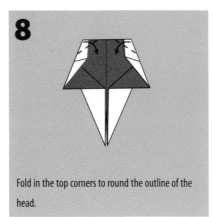

Fold in the top corners to round the outline of the head.

9

Fold the paper in half and rotate it to look like the figure in step 10.

10

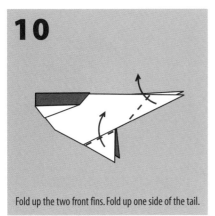

Fold up the two front fins. Fold up one side of the tail.

11

The paper will look like this. (Optional: Curl the tail.)

12

The finished Tancho Kohaku Koi.

Whether Chinese, Korean, or Japanese, Asian dragons are thought to live in the water and fly through the air. In Asian myths and traditions dragons are capable of bringing rain and creating thunder with their battles in the sky.

Dragons are often associated with themes of renewal, and perhaps for this reason the traditional Chinese New Year celebration always features the Dance of the Dragon. In this dance several people dress up in a dragon costume and dance in a human chain. Together they become a large serpentine dragon with the lead person controlling the fierce head, raising and lowering it to excite the crowd.

Use a dollar bill instead of regular origami paper to create this project. In Asia, paper money is often integrated into art or craft items that are given as gifts or religious offerings to the local Buddhist temple, and they can be disassembled when the money is needed. Paper money specially printed for the purpose is ceremonially burned as an offering to one's ancestors. It is believed that the burned money will be sent to the spirit world and to the deceased.

dollar-bill dragon

Design by Michael LaFosse, U.S.A.

What You Need

Use a crisp, new dollar bill. Other denominations are fine, too, especially if the dragon is to be a gift of money. You can fold this dragon from any rectangular strip of paper, which is a good way to practice the model before using real money. And longer rectangles make longer dragons! You can try using paper money from other countries, too.

45

What You Do

1

Fold in half, from long edge to long edge. Unfold.

2

Fold in the top and bottom corners of the right side. Be sure to align their edges with the center crease.

3

Fold out the two corner points. Make each point touch the middle of its folded edge.

4

Fold over the right corner to make the nose.

5

Your paper will look like this. Turn the paper over.

6

Fold in the top and bottom corners of the left side. Be sure to align their edges with the center crease.

7

Fold in the top and bottom edges to meet at the center crease.

8

Fold in the top and bottom angled edges of the left end to make the tail thin.

9

Fold entirely in half, from the top edge to the bottom edge.

10

Inside-reverse fold the full length of the body. Look at step 11 for the desired shape.

11

Make the body snakelike using a series of inside-reverse folds. Look at step 15 for a suggested shape, but you may make a different shape if you wish. Follow the close-up details to finish the head.

12

Pull up the triangle flaps to make the horns.

13

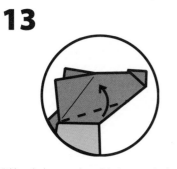

Fold up the bottom edges of the jaw to make the whiskers.

14

The finished dragon head.

15

The finished Dollar-Bill Dragon.

chinese zodiac wheel

**Design by
Michael LaFosse,
U.S.A., and
Satoshi Kamiya,
Japan**

**Inspired by designs by Paulo
Basceta, Italy, and Mette
Pederson, U.S.A.**

This project uses twelve pieces, a number that represents the animals of the Chinese zodiac. These animals are a rat, an ox, a tiger, a rabbit, a dragon, a snake, a horse, a sheep, a monkey, a rooster, a dog, and a pig. These twelve animals follow a twelve-year cycle. Discover which animal you are by finding the animal that corresponds with your birth year on page 51.

The twelve pieces of this model also represent the twelve months of the year, which makes it a great project to fold as you celebrate the new year. This project is a wonderful frame for displaying an object in its center or, if made large enough, it can be a crown for your head. When made with alternating colors, it can be an exciting composition, like dragons chasing each other, or elephants walking in circles, each joined by trunk and tail. Decorative Chinese borders and carvings around frames, windows, and doorways often have interwoven elements similar to these folded pieces.

What You Need

You will need twelve pieces of square paper, all the same size. You can make small wheels from smaller papers and large wheels from larger papers. The final size of the wheel will be the same size as the square you start with, so twelve sheets of six-inch (15 cm) paper will make a six-inch wheel. A classic color combination is red and gold, but you can try all kinds of color combinations. Try six each of two colors, four each of three colors, three each of four colors, and even twelve colors! Choose colors that represent the season or a special holiday.

What You Do

1 Begin with the white side up, if you are using origami paper. Mark the middle of the right edge of the paper by folding it in half, from bottom edge to top edge.

2 Make a short pinch fold at the right. Unfold.

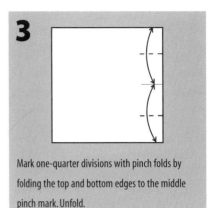

3 Mark one-quarter divisions with pinch folds by folding the top and bottom edges to the middle pinch mark. Unfold.

4 Make one-eighth divisions with pinch folds. Unfold.

5 Fold up the bottom edge to the top-most pinch mark.

6 Your paper will look like this. Unfold.

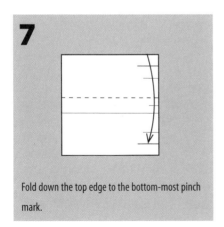

7 Fold down the top edge to the bottom-most pinch mark.

8 Your paper will look like this. Unfold and rotate the paper so that the pinch marks are at the bottom of the paper.

9 Fold the left and right top corners to the creases, each to the creases nearest to its own side. Be sure to neatly align the edges of the paper to the creases.

10

Fold up the bottom edge of the square to the bottom edges of the folded triangles.

11

Fold the bottom rectangle shape in half, from the bottom edge to the top edge.

12

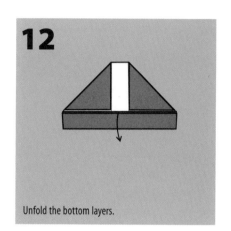

Unfold the bottom layers.

13

Bring up the bottom edge to the topmost crease. Look at step 14 for the desired shape.

14

Your paper should look like this. Turn the paper over.

15

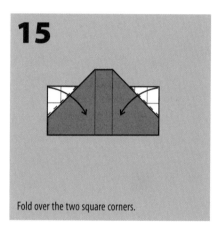

Fold over the two square corners.

16

Fold up the bottom edge, making the fold run along the bottom edges of the triangle shapes.

17

Mountain fold the center parallel creases, bending the left and the right sides so that the folded unit is square.

18

Note that each unit has two tabs (the square ends) and two pockets, one on each side.

19

When you have made two units, the tabs of one unit will slide into the pockets of the other, one on each side.

20

Push them together until they are snug. Add each new unit to the pocket end of the growing puzzle. You can use as few as nine or as many as fourteen units to make a ring. Twelve units make a great decoration for any New Year celebration.

Mouse (1948, 1960, 1972, 1984, 1996, 2008, 2020, 2032)

Dragon (1952, 1964, 1976, 1988, 2000, 2012, 2024, 2036)

Monkey (1956, 1968, 1980, 1992, 2004, 2016, 2028, 2040)

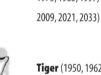
Ox (1949, 1961, 1973, 1985, 1997, 2009, 2021, 2033)

Snake (1953, 1965, 1977, 1989, 2001, 2013, 2025, 2037)

Rooster (1957, 1969, 1981, 1993, 2005, 2017, 2029, 2041)

Tiger (1950, 1962, 1974, 1986, 1998, 2010, 2022, 2034)

Horse (1954, 1966, 1978, 1990, 2002, 2014, 2026, 2038)

Dog (1958, 1970, 1982, 1994, 2006, 2018, 2030, 2042)

Rabbit (1951, 1963, 1975, 1987, 1999, 2011, 2023, 2035)

Ram (1955, 1967, 1979, 1991, 2003, 2015, 2027, 2039)

Pig (1959, 1971, 1983, 1995, 2007, 2019, 2031, 2043)

i ching wheel

**Design by
Michael LaFosse, U.S.A.**

**Inspired by designs by Paulo
Basceta, Italy, and Mette
Pederson, U.S.A.**

This project uses eight pieces, which correspond to eight-element designs that are a common theme in Chinese culture. One example is the *I Ching*, a famous book that details an ancient fortune-telling system. The book describes a ritual of drawing sticks or tossing coins to determine the ordering of broken and unbroken lines into groups of three. There are eight of these *trigrams*, and they represent the elements of Heaven, Wind, Water, Mountain, Earth, Thunder, Fire, and Lake. The trigrams are grouped into twos, in numerous combinations, to create six-lined figures called *hexagrams*, which are used to tell one's fortune.

This design was created from experimenting with the Chinese Zodiac Wheel. After playing with different widths for the pieces, we came up with this eight-element design.

What You Need

You will need eight pieces of square paper, all the same size. You can make small wheels from smaller papers and large wheels from larger papers. The final size of the wheel will be three-quarters the size of the square you start with, so a six-inch (15 cm) paper will make four-and-a-half-inch wheel. For the best results, use two different colors of paper, four pieces of each color. The wheel will look like it is made from two different colored square frames that weave through each other.

What You Do

1

Mark the middle of the right edge of the paper by folding it in half, from the bottom edge to the top edge.

2

Make a short pinch fold at the right. Unfold.

3

Mark one-quarter divisions with pinch folds by folding the top and bottom edges to the middle pinch mark. Unfold.

4

Fold up the bottom edge to the topmost pinch mark.

5

Your paper will look like this. Unfold.

6

Fold down the top edge to the bottommost pinch mark.

7

Your paper will look like this. Unfold and rotate the paper so that the pinch marks are at the top of the paper.

8

Fold the left and right top corners to the creases, each to the crease nearest to its own side. Be sure to neatly align the edges of the paper to the creases.

9

Fold up the bottom edge of the square to the bottom edges of the folded triangles.

10

Fold the bottom rectangle shape in half, from the bottom edge to the top edge.

11

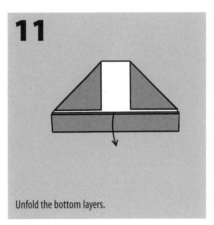

Unfold the bottom layers.

12

Neatly fold the bottom edge to the first crease from the bottom.

13

Bring up the bottom edge to the topmost crease. Look at step 14 for the desired shape.

14

Your paper should look like this. Turn the paper over.

15

Fold over the two square corners.

16

Fold up the bottom edge, making the fold run along the bottom edges of the triangle shapes.

17

Mountain fold the center parallel creases, bending the left and right sides so that the folded unit is square.

18

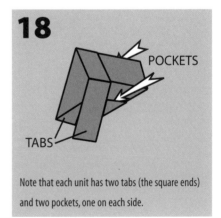

Note that each unit has two tabs (the square ends) and two pockets, one on each side.

19

When you have made two units, the tabs of one unit will slide into the pockets of the other, one on each side.

20

Push them together until they are snug. Add each new unit to the pocket end of the growing puzzle. You need a total of eight units to complete this puzzle.

crane

**Traditional
Japanese design**

The Crane represents the most popular Japanese contribution to origami. It embodies elegant lines, perfect composition, and requires the folder to achieve a certain degree of skill to produce an acceptable model.

The crane has always been an important figure in Chinese, Korean, and Japanese art for many reasons, perhaps the main reason being that they are beautiful birds with long legs, an elegant neck, a slender beak, and large, powerful wings. The crane is a symbol of peace and represents an ideal of quiet strength and beauty, fidelity and faithfulness, and patience. It is considered good luck to see a crane because they often travel great distances and could be gone for a long time.

There is an Asian legend that the crane lives for one thousand years. Since the Japanese developed the folding design for the traditional paper crane, the legend has been extended to bestow luck and good fortune on anyone who folds one thousand cranes. Certainly, when times were difficult, anyone with the luxury of enough time to fold one thousand cranes was indeed blessed.

What You Need

Use square paper of any size. Some people challenge themselves by seeing how small an origami crane can they make—the results can be microscopic!

56

What You Do

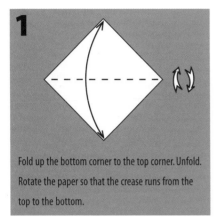

1 Fold up the bottom corner to the top corner. Unfold. Rotate the paper so that the crease runs from the top to the bottom.

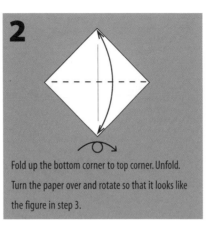

2 Fold up the bottom corner to top corner. Unfold. Turn the paper over and rotate so that it looks like the figure in step 3.

3 Fold up the bottom edge to the top edge.

4 With the folded edge at the bottom, fold in the left and the right edges to align with the angled creases. Look ahead at step 5 for the desired shape.

5 Completely unfold the paper.

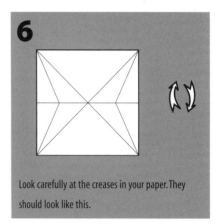

6 Look carefully at the creases in your paper. They should look like this.

7 Rotate the paper so that the central edge-to-edge crease runs from the top to the bottom. Fold up the bottom edge to the top edge.

8 With the folded edge at the bottom, fold in the left and right edges to align with the angled creases. Look ahead to step 9 for the desired shape.

9

Open the paper completely.

10

Look carefully at the creases in you paper. They should look like this.

11

Rotate your paper so that it looks like a diamond. Fold down the top corner to the bottom corner.

12

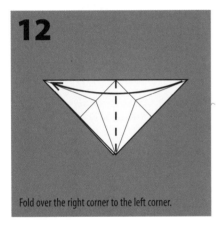

Fold over the right corner to the left corner.

13

Lift up this first layer corner. You will see that this corner has two layers of paper.

14

Open up these layers in the middle while bringing the top corner down flat.

15

Your paper will look like this. Turn the paper over, from left to right.

16

Lift up the right corner.

17

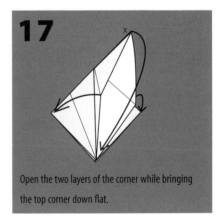

Open the two layers of the corner while bringing the top corner down flat.

18

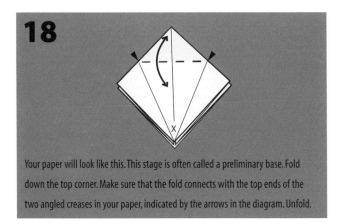

Your paper will look like this. This stage is often called a preliminary base. Fold down the top corner. Make sure that the fold connects with the top ends of the two angled creases in your paper, indicated by the arrows in the diagram. Unfold.

19

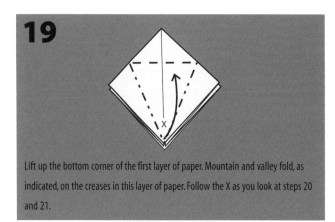

Lift up the bottom corner of the first layer of paper. Mountain and valley fold, as indicated, on the creases in this layer of paper. Follow the X as you look at steps 20 and 21.

20

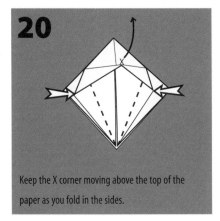

Keep the X corner moving above the top of the paper as you fold in the sides.

21

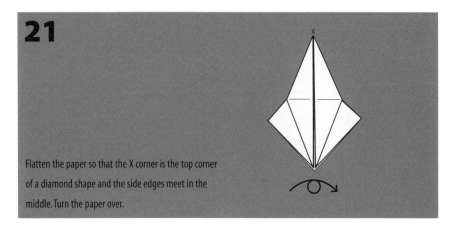

Flatten the paper so that the X corner is the top corner of a diamond shape and the side edges meet in the middle. Turn the paper over.

22

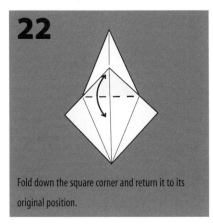

Fold down the square corner and return it to its original position.

23

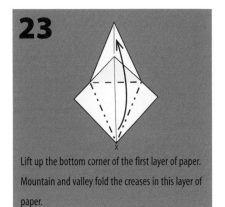

Lift up the bottom corner of the first layer of paper. Mountain and valley fold the creases in this layer of paper.

24

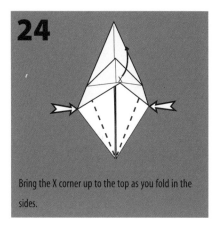

Bring the X corner up to the top as you fold in the sides.

25

X

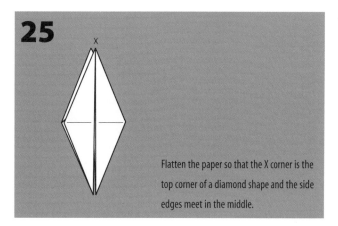

Flatten the paper so that the X corner is the top corner of a diamond shape and the side edges meet in the middle.

26

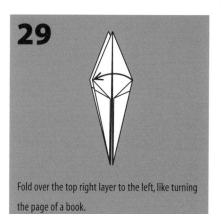

Make the split end of the diamond thinner by folding in the left and the right edges of the top layer to meet almost in the middle. Try to make good sharp points at the bottom.

27

Your paper will look like this. Turn the paper over, from left to right.

28

Fold in the left and the right bottom edges of the top layer, as you did on the other side, to make the split end thinner.

29

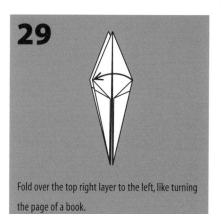

Fold over the top right layer to the left, like turning the page of a book.

30

Fold up the top layer of the bottom corner all the way to the top corner.

31

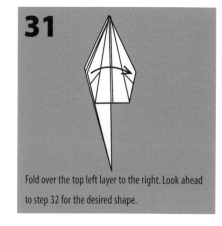

Fold over the top left layer to the right. Look ahead to step 32 for the desired shape.

32

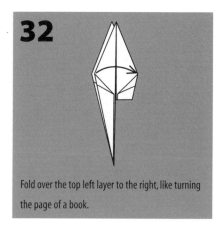

Fold over the top left layer to the right, like turning the page of a book.

33

Fold up the bottom corner all the way to the top corner.

34

Fold down the top corner of the top layer to make paper available for the head.

35

Fold over the top right layer to the left. Look ahead to step 36 for the shape.

36

Fold down the wing papers so they are flat.

37

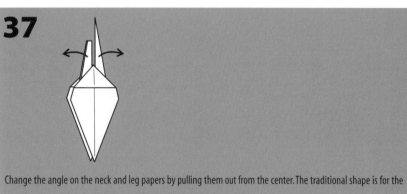

Change the angle on the neck and leg papers by pulling them out from the center. The traditional shape is for the outside folded edges to align, but you can experiment with different shapes.

38

Find the folded corner inside the neck paper and pull it out to make the beak.

39

Lift up the wings.

40

The finished Crane.

daruma

Design by
Michael LaFosse, U.S.A.

The *Daruma* is a popular toy in Japan. The toy is based on a famous Indian monk, Bodhidharma, who brought Buddhism to China over fifteen hundred years ago. One story about Bodhidharma tells how he once sat in meditation for almost ten years, his legs wasting away to nothing. So the Daruma doll resembles a red-robed monk with no legs.

The Daruma toys are always sold "eyeless" so that the person receiving the Daruma toy can make a wish by painting in one of the eyes. Legend has it that the Daruma, wanting the other eye, will help the wish to come true. In gratitude for the wish being granted, the recipient of the wish must paint in the other eye.

The Daruma doll is commonly bought at the beginning of the new year, when hope for positive change is highest.

The origami Daruma doll can be used in the same tradition: Make a wish and fold in one eye; when your wish comes true, you can fold in the other eye! This makes for a wonderful New Year activity. Make origami Darumas and mail them to your friends!

What You Need

Use square paper of any size. The traditional colors of the Daruma are red and white so ideally you should use origami paper colored red on one side and white on the other.

What You Do

1

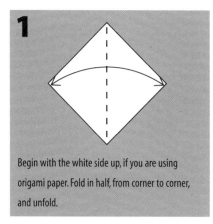

Begin with the white side up, if you are using origami paper. Fold in half, from corner to corner, and unfold.

2

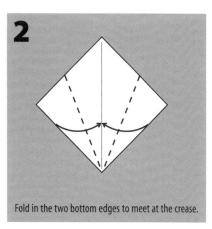

Fold in the two bottom edges to meet at the crease.

3

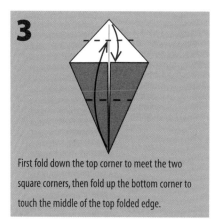

First fold down the top corner to meet the two square corners, then fold up the bottom corner to touch the middle of the top folded edge.

4

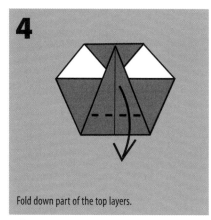

Fold down part of the top layers.

5

Fold down the top edge to meet at the level of the two square corners. Fold out the two square corners to make paper for the eyes.

6

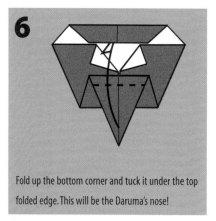

Fold up the bottom corner and tuck it under the top folded edge. This will be the Daruma's nose!

7

Your paper will look like this. Turn the paper over.

8

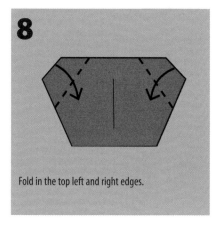

Fold in the top left and right edges.

9

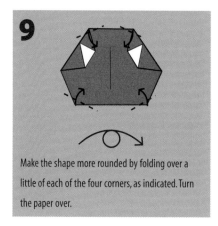

Make the shape more rounded by folding over a little of each of the four corners, as indicated. Turn the paper over.

10

The Daruma is ready to use! First, make a wish and fold over one eye corner to make the pupil show.

11

This is the Daruma doll when a wish has been made.

12

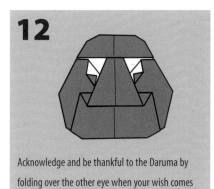

Acknowledge and be thankful to the Daruma by folding over the other eye when your wish comes true!